A BOOK OF BRITISH ECCENTRICS

RAYMOND LAMONT-BROWN

DAVID & CHARLES
Newton Abbot London North Pomfret (Vt)

British Library Cataloguing in Publication Data

Lamont-Brown, Raymond
A book of British eccentrics
1. Eccentrics and eccentricities—Great Britain—Biography
I. Title
920'.041 CT9990

ISBN 0-7153-8551-8

Typeset by Typesetters (Birmingham) Ltd, Smethwick, West Midlands
and printed in Great Britain
by A. Wheaton & Co., Hennock Road, Exeter
for David & Charles (Publishers) Limited
Brunel House Newton Abbot Devon

Published in the United States of America
by David & Charles Inc
North Pomfret Vermont 05053 USA

CONTENTS

INTRODUCING ECCENTRICITY

I come from a long line of eccentrics. My grandmother committed the greatest Victorian eccentricity of all in marrying beneath her, and was consequently 'cut off' by her family. Members of that family enjoyed royal service and had ruled over their own empire of Scottish border territory for at least a hundred years before I was born. My great-uncle, while serving as an aide-de-camp to Queen Victoria at Balmoral, had proclaimed her 'a rusty, fusty old bitch' and had retired to his estates to descend ultimately to the tomb in a veritable tide of whisky.

From time to time I feel the eccentric blood of my ancestors welling in my veins, and on such occasions allow myself a gin and tonic while soaking in the bath reading Oscar Wilde's *The Importance of Being Earnest.* Of my grandmother's children, my late father was the only one to take after her side of the family, and besides being charming to women – forsworn by his fellow-Scots as an unpardonable eccentricity – would sit in a deckchair in his declining years and shoot at pigeons with a catapult.

Despite my ancestors having diverse eccentricities, I never witnessed them personally as they had all died long before my birth, but I was introduced to eccentricity by family report. One of my distant cousins had read John Taylor's *Records of my Life* (1832) in which was the story of Dr Thomas Birch (1705–66), the historian and biographer. Cousin David was as devoted to angling as Dr Birch and had read of the worthy academic's favourite lure: the scholar used to dress in a device which made him look like a tree, his arms consequently resembling branches and his rod as a trailing spray. While Birch was ridiculed out of his activities by his friends, my cousin fell in the River Tweed too many times and declared the tree-suit unworkable.

My earliest sighting of an eccentric took place, however, when I was a schoolboy. It was my parents' custom to despatch me for the holidays to my aunt's house in a village in Berwickshire, in the Scottish Borders. There, one summer's day, I first met Erica. Erica was about sixty then and was the relict of a Calvinist minister who had given up the ghost some years earlier. Erica kept her purse in her knickers. These voluminous bloomers she would reveal every time she made a purchase. Yet, to my young mind, her greatest eccentricity of all was the flute she kept in her holdall, and while waiting in shop queues she would regale the assembled company with selections from Gilbert and Sullivan.

Once the villages, towns and cities of Britain teemed with curious folk labelled as characters, or eccentrics. Yet, as we sift through the old dickie-bird-watching photographs of these erratic dead, we look only at the eccentricity of dress and think little of the singularity of action of the sitters, and why they became eccentric at all. In some ways, the work of the modern welfare state, heralded on 1 January 1909 with the introduction of the Old Age Pension of 5s (25p) a week for all over seventy years of age, has stifled the potential of eccentricity. Again, such august bodies as the Royal Commission for the Poor Law and the Relief of Distress, and subsequent legislation, have swept away the dirt, squalor and ill-health that helped breed bizarre and abnormal behaviour. The horrors of poverty of Hanoverian, and then Victorian and Edwardian Britain – hunger, disease, overcrowding and insanitary environments being only a social crust – bludgeoned the weak and the helpless into an erratic crankiness difficult to understand today.

At street level the itinerant workers in the long-forgotten trades – knife grinders, lamp lighters, shoe blacks – rubbed shoulders with those of different eccentricity, the pursuers of middle-class social pretensions and the upper working-class obsession with 'Sunday best outfits'. (Although these classes were adhering to the rigid conventions of the time, the fact that they were 'rigid conventions' shows that so-called 'normal society' can be looked at as eccentric by succeeding generations.) While the activities of the rich and aristocratic were less socially interesting for their eccentricity – their social position gave them a kind of community licence to oddness that was accepted as a norm – it is them that we have to thank for the real birth of eccentricity.

In any survey of the convolutions of British eccentricity the diaries, journals and anecdotage of the aristocracy must figure as a prime quarry. When the aristocracy was deprived of its real power by strong monarchs like Edward I, they evolved a distinctive pattern of behaviour that set them apart from the money-grubbing merchant class. So the aristocrats set new fashions of dress, language, humour and manners which became strongly interlarded with eccentricity. Out of eccentricity, then, came escapism from the awful realities of political impotence.

For many, eccentricity became a badge and it was only a matter of time before eccentric birds of a feather flocked together. One such venue was 'The Eccentrics', a London club which first met around 1800 in a tavern in Chandos Street, Covent Garden. Afterwards its members foregathered in rooms in St Martin's Lane. Surviving until 1840, the club's membership reflected the influential social cream of the day; Charles James Fox (1749–1806), the irresponsible Whig activist, was a member, as was fellow-Whig Lord Melbourne (1779–1848), Victoria's mentor, and the unstable Lord Brougham (1778–1868).

Clearly, the dictionary definitions of 'eccentric' – 'odd, not conforming to rules, out of the usual course' – are too bland for the British character, as this book will show. Not even learned definitions, like Louis Kronenberger's in *Company Manners* (1954), come near to the British eccentric excellence: 'We might define an eccentric as a man who is a law unto himself, and a crank as one who, having determined what the law is, insists on laying it down to others.' Perhaps the true British form of eccentricity was best linked by Charles Dickens (1812–70), in *Pickwick Papers*, with genius!

RAYMOND LAMONT-BROWN
St Andrews

1

SINGULAR SOVEREIGNS

To the average foreigner – which probably includes any really nationalistic Celt of UK citizenship – HM Queen Elizabeth II (or Elizabeth I if you live in Scotland where they care about these things), the first monarch to have acceded to the throne of Great Britain and Northern Ireland while living up a tree in Africa, is the doyenne of royal eccentrics. For is it not a certain eccentricity to take your own tea, water, soap, lavatory seat, hot-water bottle and feather pillows when you go visiting? Indeed, the royal collections at the various homes of the sovereign reflect eccentric tastes, from Queen Victoria's collation of death-bed photographs of friends and servants, to HRH Prince Philip's collection of cartoons of himself hung in the lavatory at Sandringham – all following the eccentric line from Henry VIII whose most treasured possession was the left leg of St George.

Yet, for devotion to animal life in true British spirit, Henry VI bettered all for culinary eccentricity. At his coronation banquet, Lancastrian chroniclers recounted, Henry had white lions swimming in red soup, golden leopards immersed in custard and the head of a leopard crowned with ostrich feathers. King James I and VI had a different use for stags' bowels: he used to plunge his legs (James's spindly legs became too weak to carry his weight, so often courtiers had to carry him around) into pans of bowels as he averred that they strengthened the sinews.

James, incidentally, had an eccentric morbid interest in the horrible. From an early age he had an abnormal obsession for the supernatural, magic, witchcraft, freaks and monstrosities of nature. His translation of the *Furies* (a catalogue of the plagues that have beset mankind as a result of the fall of Adam and Eve) underlined James's tastes. He also wrote *Daemonologia* (to prove that witchcraft existed and that the devil was a reality) and some contemporary records note that he took part in actual witch trials in Scotland, and in the case of the North Berwick Witches (1591) personally supervised the torture of some of the accused.

One of the eccentricities of the British people is their penchant for being governed by foreigners. Because of this fondness, the early eleventh-century monarch Canute (he was also King of Denmark) was ideal. Alas, his eccentricity was that he filled his court with sycophantic half-wits who played on his gullibility. Having persuaded him that he was so marvellous, they hit the heights of fawning by persuading the old loon that he could stop the tide coming in just by commanding it to retreat. So down to the sea went Canute and dared the tide to come in. As the sea water began to rise over his Danish cross-garterings, Canute's courtiers became more and more red in the face. Eventually the dripping Canute went home to change his socks, but the precedent of having odd-ball courtiers was established.

Such a courtier was Sir Jonas More, Surveyor of the Ordnance to Charles II. Sir Jonas had peculiar tastes in drink. He wrote in a report to the king:

> The Thames Water taken up about Greenwich, at Low Water, makes very strong drink. It will of itself alone ferment wonderfully; and after its due purgations, and three times stinking (after which it continues sweet) it will be so strong that several sea commanders have told me it would burn and has often fuddled their mariners.

Sir Edward Nicholas, Secretary of State to Charles I and Charles II, noted in his papers that, on the day on which James I and VI died (27 March 1625), and in the presence of Prince Charles, the Duke of Buckingham made the late king's barber 'eat a great piece of the plaster that he had applied to King James for cure of the ague'.

For many, those imaginary lines between genius and insanity, normality and madness are very thin, so the behaviour of George III has been variously ascribed to both madness and eccentricity in various chronicles. In reality George III suffered from porphyria, a disturbance of the porphyrin metabolism (the process which gives blood its red colour) which gave him spells of delirium. The diaries of the courtiers of his day are full of the king's 'singularity'.

One such concerned meat. Whilst at Kew Palace, George III had an argument about the production of cattle. He asked: 'Why do not people plant more beef?' He was told politely that beef did not grow from seed. Not convinced, George promptly went to plant some pieces of beef-steak in his garden.

The sons of George III – Victoria called them her 'wicked uncles' – were a bizarre and motley lot, of which the seventh son, Adolphus Frederick, Duke of Cambridge, caused many a scene because of his deafness. Straining to hear, the duke sat at the front of any church he visited for divine service, and consequently was seen by the whole congregation. The embarrassment was that he made a habit of making loud comments throughout the service. When the priest said 'Let us pray', the duke would answer: 'Get on with it then!' Or, in answer to a prayer for good weather, Cambridge would mouth: 'Amen, but you won't get it till the wind drops.'

In *The Grenville Memoires* (1874–87), William IV was dismissed thus: 'What can you expect from a man with a head like a pineapple?' William succeeded to the throne with little knowledge of court etiquette when his brother George IV died. Consequently his manners in Privy Council left much to be desired – he swore lustily at his ministers – and when he decided to dissolve Parliament, went down to the House in a hackney carriage because his Master of the Horse could not get horses ready in time.

Nicknames can often reveal the eccentric habits and states of mind of our monarchs. Who but an eccentric would call his daughter Cynethrith (the name of Offa, King of Mercia's wife), or Eadgfu (Edward the Elder's wife) and Aethelflaed (Edgar's first love)? Queen Anne's nickname of 'Brandy Nan' needs no explanation, but the British do have an odd penchant for nicknaming their monarchs. Here's a few random examples: George IV was 'The Fat Adonis' and for the same reason Edward VII was called 'Tum Tum'; William II was called Rufus (he had a ruddy complexion), while Richard III was called 'Crook-back' by his enemies because of his tendency to stoop (to all kinds of skulduggery). The further we go back before micro-electronics produced an embarrassment of data on sovereigns and commoners, the eccentric nicknames told us much; for instance,

Edward II was called Edward the *Redeless*, or 'ill-counselled' because of his unfortunate habit of following loony advice.

Desperate circumstances sometimes dictate curious actions. When Richard I, by-named Coeur-de-Lion, the twelfth-century king of England, found out that the French were attacking his possessions in Normandy, he declaimed – or so William Camden said in *Remains Concerning Britain* (1674) – 'I will never turn my back till I have confronted the French.' In accord with his princely word he caused the wall in his palace at Westminster to be broken down directly towards the south (ie, facing France).

Eccentricity of dress has been the stock-in-trade of monarchy for centuries – Henry IV, for instance, seemed to favour the embroidered tablecloth as headgear – but, head and shoulders above all royal dandies was HRH George, Prince of Wales, the complex, gigantic, 'spoilt child' of George III. George's sexual tastes and opulent appetites are well enough recorded, but maybe his wife's,Caroline Amelia Elizabeth of Brunswick, are less well known. Caroline's eccentricity of dress became even more of an embarrassment to the Prince of Wales when he became king as George IV. In her memoirs La Comtesse de Boigne left this record of Caroline:

> A fat woman of fifty years of age, plump and high-coloured. She wore a pink hat with seven or eight pink feathers floating in the wind, a pink bodice cut very low, and a short white skirt which hardly came below her knees, showing two stout legs with pink top-boots; a rose-coloured sash, which she was continually draping, completed the costume.

Her husband's reactions were very understandable when news of the death of Napoleon Bonaparte (1821) was conveyed to him by a courier with the words: 'Sire, your greatest enemy is dead.' George replied: 'By God, is *she*?'

Almost two thousand years before this, the Roman historian Dio Cassius, in *Romaika*, had described the eccentric dress of another monarch, Boudicca, Queen of the Iceni of Suffolk and Norfolk. He wrote:

> She was very tall, in appearance terrifying, in the glance of her eyes most fierce, and her voice was harsh, a great mass of the tawniest hair fell to her hips; around her neck

she wore a large golden necklace; and she wore a tunic of divers colours over which a thick mantle was fastened with a brooch. This was her invariable attire!

Queen Victoria was forceful rather than cranky, but was the one British monarch who benefited from an eccentric act. James Camden Neild, an eccentric miser, left a personal fortune amounting to £250,000 to Queen Victoria when he died in September 1852. The queen spent £31,400 of it buying Balmoral as a family home.

Victoria's son Edward VII – they were the bane of each other's lives – had a quirkiness regarding the niceties of dress. He believed that to wear court dress incorrectly brought bad luck. He always kept a close watch on the master of ceremonies to make sure that he wore his badge of office correctly, for, averred the king, 'any displacement was of evil omen'. No more was he in a good mood when thirteen sat down to dine. Winston Churchill remembered how at a party at Deepdene the king steadfastly refused to lead the party in to dinner because the company was thirteen in number (Churchill's late arrival made the company up to fourteen!). Edward was much disturbed that he had accidentally sat down to dine with thirteen people at his sister's home at Friedrichshof Castle in Germany – but was relieved when his sister informed him *sotto voce* that one of the party was pregnant.

Edward forswore that his second valet, Hawkins, who made the king's bed, should turn the mattress on Fridays. From time to time Victoria's fat and fun-loving heir was troubled with omens. Edward VII's biographer, Sir Philip Magnus-Allcroft, noted how the king 'knew' that policy in Ireland would not go well when his faithful Irish terrier 'Jack' died with great suddenness.

Edward had a great horror of crossed knives on a table, and collected charms and keepsakes from wherever he went. When Sir Luke Fildes was asked to draw the king on his deathbed, he was surprised to see the bedside festooned with charms and talismans. Edward's daughter, the unmarried Princess Victoria, explained: 'The dear old thing used to think they brought him luck!'

In terms of ablutions Edward did exhibit some eccentricity, too. At Buckingham Palace and Windsor

Castle there are three basins he had installed marke
'Teeth', 'Face', and 'Hands'.

It was only to be expected that Edward would hav
people around him who were, to say the least, 'odd'
While at Christ Church, Oxford, Edward made th
friendship of Sir Henry Rawdon-Hastings (4th Mar
quess of Hastings) who breakfasted each morning o
mackerel fried in gin, caviare on toast and a bottle o
claret. Another friend was Heneage Finch-Knightle
(7th Earl of Aylesford) – nicknamed 'Sporting Joe' -
who, when bored, would order his carriage to b
driven at a gallop down Regent Street or The Strand
Aylesford would perch on the carriage roof and thro
bags of flour at pedestrians.

Queen Mary, or Victoria Mary Augusta Louis
Olga Pauline Claudine Agnes for short, had a curiou
covetous streak. Before she made a visit, the nobilit
cleared their drawing-rooms and galleries of trea
sures, for if the queen saw something she liked sh
expected it to be delivered forthwith to Sandringham

Britain can sigh contentedly that royal singularit
is in good hands for, despite Gordonstoun, trip
around the world and the Windsor family tradition o
a blanket indifference to the arts, the new Bonni
Prince Charlie is devoted to his own special collectio
of lavatory seats, of which he has some hundred.

2

ODD WISHES OF THE DEAR DEPARTED

'To my faithful goldfish, I bequeath . . .' – not so strange an entry in a will when one considers the eccentricities which have survived long after the death of the deceased. Scores of British wills and legacies mirror idiosyncrasies of the dead. The Scottish writer Robert Louis Stevenson (1850–94), had an extraordinary skill in sharing his experience and wanted to have one 'happy experience' live long after his death. He left his *birthday* to a young girl who 'was born on Christmas Day, and is therefore, out of all justice, denied the consolation of a proper birthday'.

One Englishwoman who went to live in America devised the strangest method of all to carry out her eccentric last wish. In 1937, she corked her will, bequeathing an estate of $6 million, into a bottle and flung it into the Pacific. Later recovered on a Californian beach, the document read: 'To avoid all confusion, I leave my entire estate to the lucky person who finds this bottle and to my attorney Barry Cohen, share and share alike.'

In 1788 one David Davis of Clapham, London, made his will and bequeathed, 'To Mary Davis, daughter of Peter Delaport, the sum of five shillings which is sufficient to enable her to get drunk for the last time at my expense.' He was better motivated than the butler of a Welsh landowner who left '£5 to buy oil to burn down the old b-----'s stables'. In St Mary's churchyard, Lambeth, London, is to be seen the tomb of the Tradescant family. On the tomb are carved the most extraordinary collections of objects to be seen on any metropolitan tomb. Hardly surprising indeed, for John Tradescant, who died in 1638, was one of Britain's earliest collectors of natural curiosities. Among his treasures was a 'dragon's egg' and two feathers from 'the tail of a phoenix'. On his death the collection was absorbed into that of the Ashmolean Museum, Oxford; Tradescant's bequest filled twelve carts.

Sir Nicholas Crispe's last request is still to be seen in St Paul's Church, near the Broadway, Hammersmith, London, along the west wall of the north aisle. After a lifetime of service to Charles I, Crispe wished his heart to be buried at the feet of his master. So, while Sir Nicholas's cadaver lies outside the church, his heart reposes in an urn below Le Sueur's bust of the king. Crispe's last testament noted that on the anniversary of the heart's entombment (and for a hundred years after Crispe's death) it should be removed from the urn 'and refreshed with a glass of wine'.

On the eve of Ascension Day down by the water's edge at Whitby harbour, a knot of people gather to carry out a strange ritual. Their purpose is to enact the dying testament of a Benedictine monk from the abbey on the cliffs high above the old fishing town in North Yorkshire. His deathbed instructions have to be obeyed to avoid a bizarre legal wrangle.

It appears that on 16 October 1159 a hunting party led by William de Bruce and Ralph de Percy chased a wounded wild boar into woodland owned by the abbey. A hermit monk allowed the boar into his chapel by the waters of the River Esk and gave the beast holy sanctuary. Furious, the huntsmen forced the door and, violating sanctuary, stabbed the monk with their boar staves. As he was dying, the monk proclaimed a verbal testament in which he charged his attackers (and their heirs) a yearly penance of building a hedge in Whitby harbour. If the hedge withstood the inrush of three tides the penance was served until the next year. If the heirs and successors failed, the property would be forfeit.

Today, the Hutton family have fallen heirs to the perpetual task and hold a special deed for the former abbey lands. A representative of the family builds the hedge and blows a horn to signal that the penance has been done.

For centuries people all over Britain have been buried outside churchyards for a number of odd reasons. Others have been entombed because of some eccentric whim or other. For example, they still call him 'Old Jimmy Garlick', but no one knows his real name, and for more years than any living man can tell his last resting place has been a cupboard in the church of St James, Garlickhythe, near Upper

Thames Street, London. 'Old Jimmy' first became a personality back in 1666 when the Great Fire of London gutted the church of St James, for among the smouldering ruins was found the embalmed body of this mystery man. His cadaver had been buried in a glass coffin under the high altar, but all papers and funeral bric-à-brac relating to his identity had been, presumably, burnt – and, ever since, the pious and the curious have wondered just who he was.

In 1942 'Old Jimmy' made a miraculous escape when the church received a direct bomb hit. Thereafter 'Old Jimmy' was still to be seen in his glass-fronted case to scare the daylights out of people who came across him unawares.

In the 1950s an elderly lady visited the church and told one of the church officers that she had found the will of 'Old Jimmy' and she promised to return with the proof of his identity the following Sunday, but she was never seen again. The superstitious believe that 'Old Jimmy' prefers anonymity and will do almost anything to protect it.

In Tolleridge churchyard, Hertfordshire, this slab to an unknown woman reveals how people once gave much thought to 'last requests':

> She repeatedly prayed to be evicted
> For twenty-nine years she was afflicted
> And it was her wish to be buried
> Beneath this ancient tree.

While the Victorians really made a 'spectacle' and an 'occasion' of the funeral, with people like the Reverend Patrick Brontë (father of the famous Charlotte, Emily, Anne and Patrick Branwell Brontë) requesting in his last testament to be buried in layers of charcoal, the 'last requests' of others seem today to be even more strange.

Major Peter Labillière, for instance, expressly desired to be interred on Box Hill, near Dorking, Surrey, in a grave 10ft (3m) deep, and the coffin let down in perpendicular fashion. The major's concern to be thus placed was that he would 'come right at last' if 'the world should turn topsy-turvy'.

A fig tree in the cemetery at Watford, Hertfordshire, represents quite a different request. One account of the tale tells how an atheist, when dying, ordered a fig to be placed in his mouth when he was buried, stating that if there really was a God the fig would grow. In time all the faithful around were not surprised when the tombstone split in all directions to allow the fig tree to emerge.

Hughenden churchyard, near High Wycombe, Buckinghamshire, contains another relic of a strange last request.

DIED AT HIGH WYCOMBE, BUCKS
ON THE 24TH MAY, 1837
MR JOHN GREY
AGED 64.

On the marble tombstone placed above the lid of the coffin was:

HERE WITHOUT NAIL, OR SHROUD, DOTH LIE
OR COVERED BY A PALL, JOHN GREY
BORN MAY 17TH, 1773
DIED – 24TH, 1837

In coffin made without a nail,
Without a shroud his limbs to hide
For what can pomp or show avail,
Or velvet pall, to swell the pride?
Here lies JOHN GREY beneath this sod
Who loved his friends, and fear'd his God.

A contemporary source explains:

> The grave and coffin were made under Mr Grey's own directions more than a year before his death; the inscription on the tablet, and the lines on the gravestone were his own composition, and he gave all orders respecting his funeral himself, the sum of five shillings being wrapped in separate pieces of paper for each of the bearers. The coffin was of singular beauty and neatness of workmanship, being apparently more like a piece of drawingroom furniture than a receptacle for the dead.

A youth who died from an excess of fruit pie requested that the cause of his end be engraved on stone as an example for others. His epitaph is in Monmouth churchyard, Monmouth:

Currants have check't the current of my blood,
And berries brought me to be buried here;
Pears have par'd off my body's hardihood,
And plumbs and plumers spare not one so spare.
Fain would I feign my fall! so fair a fare
Lessens not hate, yet 'tis a lesson good.

Gilt will not long hide guilt, such thinwashed ware
Wears quickly and its rude touch soon is rued.
Grave on my grave some sentence grave and terse,
That lies not as it lies upon my clay,
But in a gentle strain of unstrained verse,
Prays all to pity a poor patty's grey
Rehearses I was fruitful to my hearse,
Tells that my days are told, and soon I'm toll'd away.

Jeremy Bentham (1748–1832), 'one of the most influential men who ever lived', and the founder of Utilitarianism, a school of moral philosophy in which the ethic of the greatest possible happiness for the largest possible number of people was propounded, shocked the people of his time by suggesting that the conventional form of burial be discontinued. In its place Bentham averred that the cadavers of the deceased be preserved, and varnished against the weather, to be set up like statues in the gardens of their former homes as a permanent memorial.

This accomplished writer, chemist, botanist and musician took steps during his lifetime to be amongst those so immortalised, and his padded skeleton dressed in his own clothes and, surmounted by a replacement wax head (the original is still preserved at University College, London), still sits in a cupboard of the university he helped to found.

Another who wished to leave a testament of courage to those who might be down-heartened by infirmity, was Lucy Warner who was buried at St Giles's, Camberwell. Her epitaph reads: THE LITTLE WOMAN OF PECKHAM WHO DIED IN 1821 AGED 71, the strange story being that Lucy kept a school where all the children were taller than she was – this teacher measured only 32in (81cm) high.

A lady of letters, one Ellen Gee of Kew, Surrey, wished to offer a feast of alphabet letters to the public even up to her dying testament. This is carved on her tomb:

Peerless yet hapless maid of Q
Accomplish'd L N G
Never again shall I and U
Together sip our T.
For, ah! the fates I know not Y,
Sent 'midst the flowers a B,
Which ven'mous stung her in the I,
So that she could not C.

L N exclaim'd Vile spiteful B,
If ever I catch U
On jess'mine, rosebud or sweet P,
I'll change your stinging Q.
I'll send you, like a lamb or U
Across the Atlantic C,
For our delightful Village Q,
To distant O H I E
A steam runs from my wounded I,
Salt as the briny C,

As rapid as the X or Y,
The O I O or D
Then fare-thee-well, insatiate B
Who stung nor yet knew Y,
Since not for wealthy Durham's C
Would I have lost my I.
They bear with tears fair L N G
In funeral R A,
A clay-clod corse now doom'd to B
While I mourne her D K.
Ye nymphs of Q, then shun each B
List to the reason Y;
For should a B C U at T,
He'll surely sting U R I
Now in a grave L deep in Q,
She's cold as cold can B
Whilst robins sing upon A U
Her dirge and L E G.

3
CAPITAL CAPERS

Because of its governmental role in British society, London has witnessed the full range of eccentric folk and strange feats. Above all other quaint activities, Londoners seem to do the most curious things with food and drink, and partake of it in the oddest places.

On 23 October 1843, for instance, a few days before the statue to Horatio, Viscount Nelson, the English admiral, was erected, fourteen people ate a rump-steak dinner on top of Nelson's column in Trafalgar Square. Again, before the quadriga (a two-wheeled cart drawn by four horses abreast) was set up on the arch on top of Constitution Hill, the sculptor Adrian Jones and some friends had tea inside the horses.

London's most celebrated eighteenth-century cook, Tom Pierce, was challenged by some eccentric diners at the 'Castle', near Covent Garden, to cook a mystery item of their choice. One gentleman, not satisfied with merely drinking from a lady's shoe, had Pierce cook the shoe and serve it up for supper. Pierce did so and the man ate it!

During an evening soirée at Lady Sunderland's house in Leicester Square, in 1672, a man called Richardson astonished the company by placing a live coal on his tongue. Bowling the coal with bellows until it flamed, Richardson then cooked an oyster on it.

For a wager, James Austin, an ink manufacturer in the London of Dr Johnson, baked a plum pudding in the Thames. Austin placed the pudding mixture in a tin and put the tin into a sack of lime and lowered the whole into the Thames. Two and a half hours later he retrieved his pudding which was 'Just a little over-done'.

During the early 1560s a number of Easterlings (German immigrants) fell ill while melting metal at the Royal Mint. An apothecary suggested that they would be cured if they drank from a human skull. In those days there were plenty of human skulls to be found displayed on London Bridge. So 'cuppes' were made thereof, and 'whereof they dranke and founde some relief althoughe the mooste of them dyed'.

Early in the nineteenth century, London milk distributors noticed an enormous drop in milk consumption. The rumour had spread around the city that the erratic aristocrat William Douglas, Duke of Queensbury, was taking his daily bath in milk, and that it was being resold after he had used it. It was not until the duke died in 1810 that milk consumption in London rose again.

Should you have entered the shop of Mr Hatche, trunk maker, 404 The Strand, in 1788, you would have been invited, for the payment of 2s 6d (12½p) to see 'The Original Stone Eater'. According to advertisements in the journals of the day, the Stone Eater subsisted by eating pebbles, flints, tobacco pipes and 'mineral excrescences'. After they had been swallowed, those of strong constitution were further invited to place an ear next to the man's waistcoat to hear the stones chink in his belly.

In those days the more eccentric shopkeepers would display all kinds of bizarre desiderata. One James Salter, nicknamed 'Don Saltero', had a coffee-house at 18 Cheyne Walk, Chelsea, and displayed there 'A piece of Solomon's Temple, Job's Tears, A Curious Flea-Trap, a piece of Queen Catherine's Skin, and Pontius Pilate's wife's great-grandmother's hat'.

Ridiculous feats, too, are well recorded in London's archives. On 10 August 1749, an Islington publican called Thomas Topham amused his customers by smashing coconuts against his ear, rolling up pewter plates like paper, lifting oak tables with his teeth and heaving his horse over a turnpike gate for good measure. In 1650 a Thames waterman called John Taylor rowed from London to Queensborough (a distance of some 40 miles (64 km)) in a boat he had made from brown paper; his oars were two stockfish (of the cod family) strapped to bamboo canes.

Another dotty exploit was regularly demonstrated by Michael Boai at the Egyptian Hall, Piccadilly. At a concert at the hall on 7 June 1830 he delighted audiences by playing pieces on his chin with a hammer. Boai produced his 'music' by tapping his chin, while changing the shape of his mouth to vary the pitch.

London's only one-legged Lord Mayor, Sir Brooke Watson (he lost his leg to a shark in waters off Havana) captained a cricket team in 1796 composed of Greenwich pensioners with wooden legs, against one-armed pensioners. The match took place at Montpellier Tea Gardens, Walworth, and the Lord Mayor's team won by 103 runs (or hops).

An unintentional accomplishment, perhaps, was that achieved by Thomas Babington, 1st Baron Macaulay, the historian and statesman. Macaulay is deemed to have been the only man to walk through every street in London. One wag pointed out that (in Macaulay's day) this was equal to walking to India, a pertinent comment as Macaulay was appointed to the Supreme Council of India.

Some people have risked all for fashion. In 1797 one John Hetherington, a hatter with a shop in The Strand, was fined £500 because he wore a top hat. The court in which he was bound over to keep the peace heard how the sight of his '"tall structure of shining lustre", caused women to faint and a boy got his arm broken in the excitement'. Another, Jonas Hanway (1712–86, said to have introduced the umbrella into Britain), was called an 'extreme eccentric' because he carried an umbrella, despite the jeers and anger of the sedan chairmen and hackney coachmen (the latter believed that Hanway would ruin their trade during wet weather).

Eccentricity has often been used to 'get one's own back' on a rival. Theodore Edward Hook, the dramatist and novelist (his father wrote the famous ballad 'The Lass of Richmond Hill'), used his peculiar wit to discomfit Mrs Tottenham of 54 Berners Street in 1809. He spent five weeks writing over one thousand letters to tradesmen ordering goods to be delivered at Mrs Tottenham's on a certain day at a certain time. On the day appointed Berners Street was choked with carts, waggons and vans – from undertakers to bakers – as well as the carriages of the lord mayor and the governor of the Bank of England. The hoax was soon discovered, but Hook was never prosecuted.

Martin van Butchel was perhaps the city's most celebrated dentist in the late 1790s. His practice was in Mount Street and his eccentric ways brought him more trade than his skills. Each day he rode through Hyde Park on his pony. On the beast's forehead was a device incorporating a roller blind which van Butchel unrolled over the pony's eyes in traffic in case the animal took fright. The dentist shoed the pony himself and would not allow its mane or tail to be cut. The pony's most eye-catching features, however, were the purple designs painted on its body (van Butchel paid an artist 1 guinea (£1.05) per design to decorate the pony). Another quirky dental practitioner was Dr Monsey (1694–1788) who devised a novel method of extracting teeth while at the old College of Physicians. He tied one end of a piece of catgut around the rotten tooth and secured the other end to a bullet, which he fired from a pistol; he literally shot the tooth out.

4

WOMEN: WANTON, WILD AND WACKY

William Congreve (1670–1729), the Restoration dramatist whose witty plays include *Love for Love*, caused his erstwhile mistress, Henrietta Godolphin, Duchess of Marlborough, a problem by dying. Broken-hearted, the duchess kept Congreve's memory fresh by having a life-size model of the dramatist in wax seated in her drawing-room. The dummy (Congreve, not the duchess) was waited upon at meal-times, and as Congreve had suffered with his legs, the duchess had the model regularly treated for gout by her personal physician.

In the cemetery at Brighton, this epitaph was to be seen:

In Memory of
PHOEBE HESSEL
who was born at Stepney, in the Year 1713.
She served for many years
as a private Soldier in the 5th Regt of foot
in different parts of Europe
and in the Year 1745 fought under the command
of the Duke of Cumberland
at the Battle of Fontenoy
where she received a Bayonet wound in her Arm.
Her long life which commenced in the time of
QUEEN ANNE
extended to the reign of
GEORGE IV
by whose munificence she received comfort
and support in her later Years
she died at Brighton where she had long resided
December 12th.1821. Aged 108 Years.

According to Lewis Melville in his *Brighton: its History, its Follies, and its Fashion* (1909), she received an annuity from the then Prince of Wales (later King George IV):

> She obtained leave to sit at the corner of The Steine and the Market Parade with a little basket containing sweets,

pincushions, and toys . . . and when a grand fête was organised at Brighton to celebrate the victory at Waterloo, the ex-soldier, then one hundred and two years old, was seated, as the town's oldest inhabitant, at the Vicar's right hand.

Several women acted as soldiers and sailors in the days when it was 'eccentric' to do so. The Reverend James Woodforde in *Diary of a Country Parson* (21 May 1778), talks of Hannah Snell (1723–92) who served at the Battle of Pondicherry (1761: Seven Years' War) where the forefinger of her right hand 'was cut off by a sword'. Around 1693 one Christian Davis enlisted and ultimately served in the 2nd Dragoons (Scots Greys). Fighting bravely at the Battle of Blenheim she was undetected as a woman, but when wounded at Ramillies her sex was discovered after a surgeon had perforce to examine her. Elizabeth Bowden, described as 'a little female tar' served for many months undetected as a woman aboard the *Hazard*, while Wilhelmina (William) Brown, a negress, served as a naval rating for eleven years aboard the *Queen Charlotte* and became 'Captain of the Main Top'. Formidable women all, but none more obsessive about hiding her sex than Dr James Barry.

Under the title of 'A Strange Story', this appeared in the *Manchester Guardian* of 21 August 1865:

> Our officers quartered at the Cape between 15 and 20 years ago may remember a certain Dr. Barry attached to the medical staff there, and enjoying a reputation for considerable skill in his profession . . . he died about a month ago, and upon his death was discovered to be a woman.

Barry had been born around 1795 at London, of unknown parentage, which added to the mystery. It has been suggested that she was the illegitimate offspring of some English nobleman, some even whispered of the Prince Regent himself, or his brother the Duke of York. These tales appeared to have no real foundation, but the strange James Barry had a protector in the pompously capricious David Erskine, 11th Earl of Buchan. It appears that Barry entered the medical school at Edinburgh at a remarkably early age and passed out with great honour – a feat not easily achieved as the written and oral work had to be carried out in impeccable Latin.

Dr Barry served in the army as a surgeon in England, South Africa and the West Indies. How she kept her sex secret among so many men, living communally with them, remains a mystery. After a life of adventure and excitement, Barry retired to the West Indies and latterly took up residence at 14 Margaret Street, Marylebone, London.

During the uncommonly hot summer of 1865 an epidemic of diarrhoea hit London and in the third week of July 261 people died, one of the victims being Dr James Barry. On the 26 July, Henry Durham, registrar of the Marylebone district, issued a death certificate stating that on the previous day, one James Barry, Inspector General of Military Hospitals, had died and to the statement was added the mark of one Sarah Bishop who had been present at the death. The official records underlined complete normality. Soon, however, an entirely different story was being told in the clubs and parlours of London. The London papers were curiously silent on the subject; no obituary notice appeared for such a high-ranking officer, and the impression was strong that pressure was brought from 'a high authority' to kill off publicity. Yet an Irish newspaper, *Saunders's News Letter*, broke the silence:

> Very probably this discovery [that Barry was a woman] was elicited during the natural preparations for interment, but there seems to be an idea prevalent that either verbally . . . or by written [document] that he [Barry] had begged to be buried without post mortem . . . it was equally beyond doubt that the individual in question had, at sometime or another been a mother.

The charlady of the premises in Marylebone gave further testimony that 'she had examined the body and that it was a perfect female and further that there were marks on her *(striae gravidarum)* of having a child when young'. During the last years of her life Dr Barry is known to have been attended by a negro servant; she had kept a dog, and a box of family papers guarded diligently. On her death a strange footman in livery collected the box of papers, paid off the servant and took the dog away. So the mystery of the eccentric Dr Barry's birth, her child and her obsession went with her to her grave in Kensal Green.

Another woman not to be tangled with was the mother of Sir John Killigrew, Vice-Admiral of Cornwall to Elizabeth I. She commanded a boat load of rascally seamen and assaulted a Spanish merchantman in 1582. Quite often court appearances unmasked eccentric women who 'played men'. Such was the case of Elizabeth Taylor, who on 17 May 1885 appeared in a London magistrate's court for being drunk and disorderly. She had been employed, it was found, as a sailor for thirteen years and had voyaged regularly between Wales and North America.

A man, of course, could get rid of a quirky wife by dint of an odd British custom. For a hundred years before the Matrimonial Causes Act of 1857, men of small financial means (ie, they could not afford a divorce) took to selling their wives at village fairs and town crosses, sometimes for a few pence. Yorkshire was one place where this peculiar custom took place. A Halifax newspaper contained this comment: 'On Saturday, November 30th, 1833, Samuel Hey, of Midgley, sold his wife at the Market Cross, Halifax, to a neighbour for ten shillings, throwing back sixpence for luck. The town authorities resolved to take legal proceedings against him.' At Carlisle on 7 April 1832, Joseph Thomson sold his wife by auction to Henry Mears for £1 and a dog.

One strange lady, who had a fortune of £200,000, was Margaret Wharton (1688–1791), one of the Whartons of Skelton Castle in Cleveland. She always bought 'a pennyworth' of anything she wanted, and she paid cash as she 'had an aversion to tradesmen's bills'. A particular penchant of hers was eels; and when she purchased her 'pennyworth' of eels she placed them live in her pocket. She delighted in entering a carriage with the creatures wriggling in her pocket and proclaiming to all seated therein that she had her pockets full of adders – that way she got the carriage to herself. Miss Wharton was satirised as 'Peg Pennyworth' by the dramatist Samuel Foote (1720–77).

Helena, Comtesse de Noailles (1824–1908), was an English divorcee with a passion for indulging her own whims. One remarkable caprice was her purchase (for two bags of gold) of a Spanish girl called Maria Pasque in 1865. The Comtesse, who was a health freak, sent the nine-year-old Maria to a convent chool at St Leonards, Sussex, and insisted that the hild be shielded from all germs. This included the raining of the school pond ('a dangerous breeding round for insects') and giving the child milk from a ow the Comtesse bought and approved as healthy. oung Maria was also only taught subjects of which he Comtesse approved.

A diet of soft herring roe, averred the Comtesse, vas a sure cure for bronchitis, and she herself warded ff disease by wearing a stocking stuffed with grey quirrel fur around her forehead when she retired for he night. Cows were kept near to her windows, too, s she believed that the inhalation of the gas from ows' farts to be efficacious to those with weak chests.

Madame la Comtesse lived to be eighty-four and atterly only partook of milk and champagne. She left 100,000 and eleven wills to task the patience of her eirs.

Another outdoor eccentric was Baroness Sackville vho took to eating her meals alfresco despite the veather. She was undaunted by snow drifting on her utlery, or rain diluting her coffee. Even so, the eauties of nature were nothing to her as she referred tin delphiniums and porcelain daffodils which never faded nor were bothered by slugs. The llegitimate child of a Latin dancer and an English liplomat, Victoria-Josefa Sackville-West, Baroness Sackville (1862–1936), was a wealthy woman, yet purloined hotel notepaper for her personal missives and once wrote a letter on a slice of cooked ham. She even recommended the toilet paper from Harrod's ladies' room to her daughter (the writer Vita Sackville-West) as the best for retaining ink. Her fetish for postage stamps knew no bounds when she was decorating. One room of her stately home at Knole, Kent, was papered with them. She spent hours cutting up postage stamps and pasting non-franked bits together to avoid the cost of postage. During World War I, the Baroness berated Lord Kitchener (Secretary of War) that the hostilities were taking all of her servants away.

When Miss Hannah Beswick of Cheetwood Hall, Manchester, died in 1758, aged seventy-eight, she made an eccentric doctor a wealthy man. Throughout her life the odd Miss Beswick shared Edgar Allan Poe's fear of premature burial. So she left to her physician Dr Charles White the sum of £25,000 on condition that he paid regular visits to her unburied cadaver. On her death, then, Dr White had Miss Beswick embalmed and he placed her in a grandfather-clock case in her house. On the anniversary of her death, Dr White paid a visit to examine Miss Beswick's body and had his visit confirmed by a witness.

White died in 1813 and Miss Beswick was moved to Manchester's Lying-in Hospital, and later to the Manchester Museum of Natural History. When the museum was transferred to its new buildings the trustees examined Miss Beswick, declared her dead, and on 22 July 1868 she was buried in Manchester General Cemetery in an unmarked grave.

A footnote to female eccentricity is relevant in the curious activities of a person by-named 'Le Chevalier D'Eon'. He has been called 'the greatest female impersonator' who ever lived and from 1785 onwards he always dressed as a woman. Indeed, over £120,000 was wagered in London clubs on the identity of his sex. D'Eon served as a temporary ambassador of Louis XV to George III during the peace negotiations of 1761, and was decorated for his service. It was not until D'Eon died in Bloomsbury in 1810 that his sex was confirmed – the most surprised person being his housekeeper of many years who had always thought she was employed by a woman.

5

ADVERTISING ABSURDITIES

'Promise, large promise,' wrote Samuel Johnson in *The Idler, No. 1*, 'is the soul of an advertisement.' An unusual aspect of the British character – phlegmatism, dullness and stolidness being only the crust – is to be found in advertising, for from an anonymous box number the British have long flaunted their eccentricities, or even the results of their weaknesses.

Victorian publications were full of advertisements for tracts such as: *A Practical Essay on the Debilities of the Generative System*, or '*Manhood: the cause of its Premature Decline with Plain Directions for its perfect Restoration*'. Next to Wray's Balsamic Pills, 'a certain cure for gonorrhoea', would be placed advertisements for 'helpful' magazines such as *The Aegis of Life*, a comprehensive physiological history of manhood and its decay owing to the progress of self-abuse, intemperance, or debility.

Young men could be very bold in print, as witness the advertisement in the *London Chronicle* of 5 August 1758:

> A young lady who was at Vauxhall on Thursday night last, in company with two gentlemen, could not but observe a young gentleman in blue and gold-laced hat, who, being near her by the orchestra during the performance, especially the last song, gazed upon her with the utmost attention. He earnestly hopes (if unmarried) she will favour him with a line directed to A.D. at the bar of the Temple Exchange Coffee-House, Temple-bar, to inform him whether fortune, family, and character, may not entitle him upon a further knowledge, to hope an interest in the heart. He begs she will pardon the method he has taken to let her know the situation of his mind, as being a stranger, he despaired of doing it any other way, or even of seeing her more. As his views are founded upon the most honourable principles, he presumes to hope the occasion will justify it, if she generously breaks through this trifling formality of the sex, rather than, by a cruel silence, render unhappy one who must ever expect to continue so if debarred from a nearer acquaintance with her, in whose power alone it is to complete his felicity.

Vauxhall Gardens, by the by, the once famous herbaries in London's Lambeth, opened 1661 and closed 1859, were the haunts of Britain's most famous society eccentrics.

The following advertisements show a variety of British eccentricity in print:

A colourful young man
If any one can give notice of one Edward Perry, being about the age of eighteen or nineteen years, of low stature, black hair, full of pockholes in his face; he weareth a new gray suit trimmed with green and other ribbons, a light Cinnamon-coloured cloak, and black hat, who ran away lately from his Master; they are desired to bring or send word to Tho. Firby, Stationer, at Gray's Inne Gate, who will thankfully reward them. (*Mercurius Politicus*, 1 July 1658)

A medicine bag
Small baggs to hang about Children's necks which are excellent both for the prevention and cure of the Rickets, and to ease children in breeding of Teeth, are prepared by Mr Edmund Buckworth, and constantly to be had at Mr Philip Clark's, Keeper of the Library in the Fleet, and nowhere else, at 5 shillings a bagge. (*The Intelligencer*, 16 October 1664)

Decidedly dead
Whereas an ignorant Upstart in Astrology has publicly endeavoured to persuade the world that he is the late John Partridge, who died the 28 of March 1718, these are to certify all whom it may concern, that the true John Partridge was not only dead at that time, but continues so to the present day. Beware of counterfeits, for such are abroad. (*The Tatler*, 24 August 1710)

Choose your weapons
CHALLENGE – I, Elizabeth Wilkinson, of Clerkenwell, having had some words with Hannah Hyfield, and requiring satisfaction, do invite her to meet me upon the stage, and box me for three guineas; each woman holding half-a-crown in each hand, and the first woman that drops the money to lose the battle.

To which came the answer:

I, Hannah Hyfield, of Newgate Market, hearing of the resoluteness of Elizabeth Wilkinson, will not fail, God Willing, to give her more blows than words, desiring home blows, and from her no favour: she may expect a good thumping. (*The Postman*, 4 July 1701)

Blackwood's Magazine published one of the earliest lonely hearts' advertisements in Britain in the mid-1840s:

MATRIMONIAL ADVERTISEMENT – I hereby give notice to all unmarried women, that, I, John Hobnail, am at this writing five-and-forty, a widower, and in want of a wife. As I wish no one to be mistaken, I have a good cottage, with a couple of acres of land, for which I pay 2l. a year. I have five children, four of them old enough to be in employment; three sides of bacon, and some pigs ready for market. I should like to have a woman fit to take care of the house when I am out. I want no second family. She may be between forty and fifty if she likes. A good sterling woman would be preferred, who would take care of the pigs.

A hasty enquiry in The Times
TO P.Q. HOW IS YOUR MOTHER? I shan't inquire further, and must decline entering upon the collateral branches of the family

Buy a title through The Times
THE TITLE OF AN ANCIENT BARON. Mr George Robins is empowered to SELL the TITLE and DIGNITY of a BARON. The origin of the family, its ancient descent, and illustrious ancestry, will be fully developed to those and such only as desire to possess this distinguished rank for the inconsiderable sum of 1000 pounds. Covent Garden Market. (1841)

Cheap wallpaper
A young lady, being desirous of covering her dressing-room with cancelled POSTAGE STAMPS, has been so far encouraged in her wish by private friends as to have succeeded in collecting 16,000! These, however, being insufficient, she will be greatly obliged if any good-natured persons who may have these (otherwise useless) little articles at their disposal would assist in her whimsical project. (*The Times*, 1841)

6

HORSEMEN AND MEN WHO WERE HORSES

One sunny day in June 1795 two mighty eccentrics of muscle forgathered in the courtyard of the Crown Inn, Fakenham, Norfolk. Ned Denny, known as the Norfolk Samson, and Seth Blowers, the Suffolk Giant, were to take part in one of the world's most bizarre duels. Aiding and abetting them were two unconventional gamblers, Sir Harry Vernon for Ned, and Lord Beauchamp for Seth. The idea was that the 17 stone (108kg) Ned would pull a coach bearing Sir Harry, plus 9 friends, some 10 miles (16km) to the Royal George Inn. Meanwhile Seth would run with Lord Beauchamp on his back.

From the first Seth, 6ft 10in (2.08m) with bulging muscles, streaked ahead, and at the first mile (1.6km) was 50yd (48m) in front of Ned. At Walsingham, the halfway mark, Ned passed Seth, but further on when they had a 5 minute breather, they were neck-and-neck.

At the restart, Seth took the lead again, while Ned toiled behind with the full coach. Still, over the next 2 miles (3.2km) Ned even managed to pass Lord Beauchamp's panting 'mount'. By this time both men were spent, and the greatest test was ahead. About ½ mile (0.8km) from the finish lay a fairly steep hill, but once climbed it was a 50yd (48m) slope to the Royal George. At the top of the hill Seth Blowers faltered and nearly fell, but making a supreme effort he stumbled his way down the hill, only to be passed by the coach careering down with a dead Ned Denny between the shafts. Seth Blowers crossed the line and then collapsed; he, too, died three days later. Never before, nor since, has such an eccentric duel fired the imagination so much.

One man who ate like a horse was Daniel Lambert, a 52 stone (330kg) joker from Leicester. The keeper of the city prison at Leicester, Lambert was fond of a wager and challenged any man to race him – he boasted that he could beat any fit man provided he had the right to choose the course. When the wager was fixed, Lambert would take his opponent into a long, narrow passage and romp home safe in the knowledge that no one could pass one of his girth in such a confined space. Lambert died in 1809 aged thirty-nine, and was buried in St Martin's churchyard in a huge coffin that was itself pushed along on wheels – it was finally rolled down the slope into the grave.

No British horseman was stranger than Squire John Mytton of Halston, Shrewsbury. Mytton was the most reckless horseman of all time, rushing fences, scattering crowds (he used to dismount and fight with anyone who complained) and galloping across gardens. He was even more dangerous when he drove his horses at full gallop in his tandem; his eccentric efforts often included trying to get two horses and a gig over a turnpike gate unscathed (he never achieved it).

If when out hunting or racing, Mytton should get soaked with rain or ditch water, he would stop and help himself to clean clothes from washing lines irrespective of the sex of the owners (his own clothes were always the shabbiest). He used to barge into any cottage he fancied to get dry, and he insisted that his horse go in with him.

Despite his reckless life, Mytton received his worst injuries in his bed through brandy and pyrotechnics. Because of his excessive drinking, Mytton suffered from hiccups. One night he set fire to his nightshirt to frighten the hiccups away. He was drastically successful. Friends managed to put him out, but the mad squire was incapacitated for four months.

It is estimated that Mytton ran through £1 million in his short lifetime. He kept 2,000 dogs and 60 cats (each dressed in a style reflecting its breed), and his wardrobe contained 3,000 shirts, 1,000 hats and 152 pairs of trousers. At length, with all his money gone, Mytton was confined in the King's Bench Prison, where he died from delirium tremens (a wandering of the mind produced by over-absorption of alcohol) in March 1834, aged thirty-eight.

For his trade Jeremy Hirst of Rawcliffe, Yorkshire, was a tanner, and his love of horses was clearly shown by the loving care he took with horse caparisons. Yet

Jeremy was a mystery to most who met him (including George III) for his inventive mind was mirrored in his weird clothes and curious means of transport. A favourite garb he wore as he drove to Doncaster races in his wicker carriage at the turn of the nineteenth century turned many a head of those unable to resist another view of the lambskin cap of 9ft (2.7m) circumference, the otter-skin coat, the waistcoat of drake's feathers, the patchwork breeches and the red and white stockings above the bright yellow boots.

Hirst was able to indulge his fancies from profits he made from land speculations and had his own hunting pack. To the hunt he rode his favourite steed, his bull Jupiter, and at his heels scampered his 'hounds', a pack of pigs. His house was decorated with discarded farm implements from scythes to plough shares, and guests were helped to bumpers of wine which he kept in a reared-up coffin. In 1829 Hirst died and was borne to the grave in the very same coffin by 'eight portly widows' (he had wanted twelve old maids to do the job, but only two could be found), leaving Rawcliffe a much less colourful place at his passing.

Sir Walter Scott, one of literature's greatest bores if he put his mind to it, once reviewed a book on sportsmanship in the Scottish Highlands by one Colonel Thomas Thornton of Yorkshire, and dismissed it as the most boring book he had ever read. Thornton was certainly worthy of such an epithet as boring, but was given more by his neighbours who declared him a monumental liar and an accomplished 'capper'. That meant that whatever story was told, Thornton could 'cap' it. No horseman outrode Thornton, no steeplechaser outjumped him, and no one ever had an injury in the sporting field to outdo Thornton – at least in his imagination! A friend once told Colonel Thornton that a mutual acquaintance had been thrown while hunting and had a broken head.

'Broken head!' exclaimed the colonel. 'No one ever had such a broken head as I. Once when I was hunting, my mare threw me on to a scythe. My head was cut completely in two and each side lay on my shoulders!'

The dignity and style of the lord provost of Edinburgh is centuries old, the title of Edinburgh's 'chief magistrate' going back to 1667 when Charles II raised the office above that of 'common provost' (the

English equivalent is 'mayor'). So, needless to say, the corporate pride of the city was dented when a scruffy eccentric called James Duff earned the nickname of 'Lord Provost', or 'Bailie' (a city magistrate) for his mock garb of brass chain of office, cocked hat and wig. But worse was to follow. Duff regularly entered himself in the Leith horse-races as a horse. Lining up with the mounted nags, Duff would run the course barefoot, and half bending over, would whip himself with a switch. Edinburgh Town Council gave a combined municipal sigh of relief when Duff expired in 1788.

7

QUAINT CLERGY

Some clergymen have gone to great lengths to protect and endow their churches. Few, however, pulled out all stops like the Reverend George Whitefield to assure his church's legal consecration. When Whitefield built his tabernacle in Tottenham Court Road, London, in the eighteenth century, he was unable to get his graveyard consecrated in the orthodox way. So the resourceful Whitefield obtained a cart load of the top soil from a city churchyard and spread it over the ground around his church, thereby giving it a skin-deep consecration.

The Reverend Robert Stephen Hawker (1804–75) is remembered in the annals of the Church of England as the cleric who 'invented' the custom of harvest festivals. Hawker held the first harvest festival at Morwenstow, Cornwall's most northerly parish, in October 1843. Despite this piece of note-worthy ritual, Hawker must enter the annals too, as the Church of England's strangest clerk in holy orders.

As a boy in Stratton, Stephen Hawker was mischievous. When the local doctor found his horse painted with zebra stripes he knew it was Hawker he had to seek for a confession. Such havoc did he wreak in the north Cornish town that when he went to boarding school, the parish clerk rang a peal of church bells to rejoice.

When a financial disaster looked like ruining his further education, Hawker married his godmother (a woman older than his mother) to ensure a source of money. Despite his practical jokes and hoaxes, Hawker had great intellectual ability. He shone academically at Pembroke College, Oxford, (he carried off the Newdigate Prize in 1827) and wrote the famous Cornish song based on the old ballad 'And shall Trelawny die!'

Ordained in 1831, Hawker was given the living of Morwenstow by Bishop Phillpotts, and soon set about building a new vicarage. The site he chose was where he had seen sheep sheltering during a storm. Over the main door of the vicarage, Hawker placed these lines:

A House, a Glebe, a Pound, a Day,
A Pleasant Place to Watch and Pray,
Be True to Church – Be Kind to Poor,
O Minister! for evermore.

Needless to say, the vicarage reflected Hawker's individuality. Five of its chimneys are in the shape of church spires he liked, and the sixth is in the shape of his mother's tomb.

Hawker practised what he preached and his generosity often got him into financial embarrassment. Yet he was loved by his parishioners who saw goodness in their parson who invariably dressed like a fisherman in jersey and sea-boots, and had cats on his pulpit. Fond of outrageous dress, a favourite garb too, was a purple coat, blue jersey, scarlet gauntlets and yellow poncho. Hawker was one of the first vicars in the Church of England to wear the cassock – naturally!

Many parishioners remember the Reverend Frederick William Densham, Rector of Warleggan, Bodmin, in the diocese of Truro. Inducted in 1931, Densham, over the years, quarrelled with almost every one of his parishioners when he painted his thirteenth-century church red and blue, with black and white pillars. To replace his dwindling congregation the rector placed a cardboard cutout with name-card in each vacant seat.

As he never visited his parishioners, or ventured into Warleggan, Densham discouraged visitors with an 8ft (2.4m) barbed-wire fence around his rectory, and provided boxes for mail and provisions deliveries. Until his death in 1953, Densham appeared to live on nettles and porridge, and chose to have no furniture. The rectory garden was full of children's roundabouts and games, but no children ever used them.

Like Densham, several of Britain's clergymen down the centuries have shown very eccentric tastes when it has come to church decoration. Experts have averred that at least six churches in Britain have doors covered with human skin – they are the parish churches of Hadstock, Copford and Castle Hedingham, in Essex. Not to be outdone, the Deans of

Rochester, Winchester and Westminster, too, went in for human hide door coverings.

Those clergymen who were not getting enough attention to their sermons could take definite action. Money was raised to employ a 'sluggard-waker' in churches like that at Claverley, Shropshire. Such a church officer patrolled congregations at sermon times and rapped on the head (with a long pole) all those who had fallen asleep. At least women did not have their coiffeurs disturbed, or hats crumpled by such a means – they were tickled under the nose with a fox's brush.

How the parishioners of the Reverend John Mawer of Middleton Tyas, in the old North Riding of Yorkshire, must have groaned when he got to his feet. Mawer loved words more than people and taught himself twenty-two languages. Regularly he droned on, giving sources for the words he used until his congregations were sound asleep – so deep in vocabulary was the vicar that he seldom noticed when his congregation walked out.

One eighteenth-century clergyman, Reverend Francis Waring, vicar of Heybridge, Essex, had a penchant for rapid services. Each Sunday he placed a small timepiece on his pulpit and conducted the service at high speed. Not giving his congregation time to make responses, the vicar raced through the sermon – not much longer than a maxim – and running down the aisle he leapt on to his horse and galloped off to take services at two nearby churches.

A snappy dresser – Waring often dressed as a Quaker – the clergyman was popular for his humour, but living with him must have been a strain. He insisted that every house in which he lived should have a central passage. This passage was constructed to be so narrow that it only allowed for one person at a time. Again, though not poor, Waring insisted that his family sat on rough logs rather than chairs. His children fed from a trough and were summoned to the table, and their household tasks, with individual bird calls. The vicar and his wife slept in a huge wicker rocking-cradle.

Perhaps the most miserly clergyman in Britain was the Reverend Morgan Jones (1781–1824) of Blewby, near Didcot, Oxfordshire. His money-grubbing was inventive and he invariably dined at the expense of others. It is known that Jones wore the same coat and hat for forty-three years (he repaired his clothes with rags removed from scarecrows). His sermons were written on scraps of paper from sand-paper to used marriage licences. He left the modern equivalent of £100,000.

Canon William Buckland (1784–1856), Dean of Westminster, and Oxford's first Professor of Geology, had a life-style which, to say the least, was 'unorthodox'. He was never backward in expressing his forthright opinions and shocked many a fellow cleric. On a visit to St Rosalia's shrine at Palermo, Sicily, Buckland eyed the blood of the martyr – splattered on the pavement and deemed ever fresh and ineradicable – dropped on one knee and touching the stain with his tongue declared it to be 'bat's urine'.

Buckland was not always noted for the clarity of his thought, as Philip Shuttleworth (1782–1842) noted:

> Some doubts were once expressed about the Flood,
> Buckland arose, and all was clear as – mud.

Yet whosoever met the quirky clergyman were impressed by his individuality – not difficult with a man who averred that he had eaten his way through all known zoological specimens. Buckland thought that the nastiest food he had ever consumed was mole, but finally settled on bluebottles as the worst. Writing in *Reminiscences of Oxford* (1900) of a visit to the Buckland home, William Tuckwell remembered:

> . . . the entrance hall with its grinning monsters on the low staircase, of whose latent capacity to arise and fall upon me I never quite overcame my doubts; the side-table in the dining-room covered with fossils, 'Paws off' in large letters on a protecting card; the very sideboard candlesticks perched on saurian vertebrae; the queer dishes garnishing the dinner table – horseflesh I remember more than once, crocodile another day, mice baked in batter on a third day – while the guinea-pig under the table inquiringly nibbled at your infantine toes, the bear walked round your chair and rasped your hand with file-like tongue, the jackal's fiendish yell close by came through the open window . . .

Another who remembered Buckland's curious tastes and opinions was John Henry Newman

(1801–90). Born to be a cardinal, Newman was one of the most eminent and controversial clerics of his century. His influence was spread far beyond his country, yet even he was considered an 'eccentric' by eccentrics like Buckland on the subject of sexuality. As a general rule Britons have looked upon celibacy as odd, so Newman's decision (at fifteen) to be a celibate, in his *Apologia pro vita sua*, was deemed eccentric behaviour – a trait underlined on Newman's death by his request to be buried in the same grave as his erstwhile friend Father Ambrose St John.

Victorian England threw up a wide variety of eccentric clerics, and in the minds of the readers of the 'yellow press', none was more so than the Reverend Charles Lutwidge Dodgson (1832–98), a shy mathematics don who spent his adult days in comparative obscurity at Christ Church, Oxford. Under the pseudonym of Lewis Carroll, Dodgson won international immortality with his *Alice's Adventures in Wonderland* and *Through the Looking Glass*. Prurient Victorian society saw his hobby of 'collecting' little girls as an aberration. It was said in social circles that when Queen Victoria informed Dodgson that she had enjoyed his *Alice* very much, he delightedly sent her a copy of a predecessor work, *A Syllabus of Plane Algebraical Geometry*.

Dodgson was a keen photographer (at least until 1880 when he stopped photography for good, without explanation) and was obsessive in taking pictures of girls bare-legged (or even bare everywhere), or dressed as boys. Such subject matter was regarded by Victorians as risqué and somewhat bizarre (as several of the children were dressed theatrically). Yet it is more than speculation that physiological and psychological eccentricities may arise from genius. Dodgson certainly had a genius for bizarre humour and wrote this, 'Brother and Sister', at the age of thirteen:

'Sister, sister, go to bed!
Go and rest your weary head.'
Thus the prudent brother said.

'Do you want a battered hide,
Or scratches to your face applied?'
Thus his sister calm replied.

'Sister, do not raise my wrath.
I'd make you into mutton broth
As easily as kill a moth!'

The sister raised her beaming eye
And looked on him indignantly
And sternly answered, 'Only try!'

Off to the cook he quickly ran
'Dear Cook, please lend a frying-pan
To me quickly as you can.'

'And wherefore should I lend it you?'
'The reason, Cook, is plain to view.
I wish to make an Irish stew.'

'What meat is in that stew to go?'
My sister'll be the contents!'
'Oh!'
'You'll lend the pan to me, Cook?'
'No!'

MORAL: Never stew your sister – all making a background for the eccentric masterpiece of *Alice.*

8
PARLIAMENTARIAN FADS

Many would say that a desire to be a Member of Parliament is in itself an eccentricity. Certainly the 'Mother of Parliaments' produces behaviour that any foreigner would call eccentric. MPs, for instance, bow when leaving the floor of the House in deference not to the Speaker, but to the altar which used to be in St Stephen's Chapel. Again, the floor of the House has its own 'sacred no-man's land'; the carpet separating the Government from 'Her Majesty's Loyal Opposition' retains its width as being wide enough to prevent opposing Members from lacerating each other with swords.

Only the British with their eccentric tastes would have had a doorkeeper in charge of a snuffbox out of which Members could take a sniff at will (Members are not allowed to smoke or indeed, burst into flames in the House). At the close of each sitting a policeman is heard to shout: 'Who goes home?' This odd custom dates from the time when Members would gather together in groups to be accompanied home by armed guards to protect them from footpads and highwaymen. Today, too, the cloakroom pegs are still hung with red tapes once used for hanging up swords, but now used for umbrellas.

Alexander Cruden was an 'election freak' with a strange mission. He called himself 'Alexander the Corrector' and carried with him, at election time, a wet sponge with which to rub out election slogans chalked on walls. An eccentric Scot born in 1701, Cruden became a bookseller to Queen Anne (after he had been let out of an asylum) and completed his *Complete Concordance to the Holy Scriptures of the Old and New Testament* which appeared in 1737.

Down the centuries the voters of Britain have elected some peculiar people. One such was John Fuller (1757–1834), known to his detractors as 'Mad Jack', and to his friends as 'Honest Jack'. Fuller represented the long-defunct constituency of Rose

Hill, Sussex, from 1801 to 1812, and won the reputation of being a fiery politician. Fully 22 stone (140kg) Jack 'Hippo' Fuller more than once caused an uproar in the House with his behaviour and rhetoric and had to be forcibly ejected. Nevertheless, he had much compassion for those without a job and had high walls built around his home to provide work for those unemployed.

A number of parliamentary offices and procedures only underscore the visitor's belief that British eccentricity is to be found at all levels. Visitors – those from abroad and north of Watford – when questioned, noted the following as the most 'picturesque'.

The personage of Black Rod (really Gentleman Usher of the Black Rod) underlines for many the oddness of the House's officers. He (it is still not unisex) is a senior parliamentary official appointed by the Queen, who carries out in the House of Lords duties similar to the Serjeant at Arms in the House of Commons. The latter official, also appointed by the Queen, acts under the authority of the Speaker and is responsible for the management of the Commons area of the Palace of Westminster. The Serjeant (or one of his deputies) sits at the 'Bar of the House', and precedes the Speaker carrying the Mace on his shoulder. At the beginning of each sitting the Speaker processes from his house to the Chamber. At the annual Opening of Parliament, Black Rod is despatched to the Commons to call the MPs to attend the Queen's Speech (ie, written for her by the government of the day, outlining said government's policy for the ensuing session). Both the Serjeant at Arms and Black Rod are members of the Queen's Household under the jurisdiction of the Lord Chamberlain.

The Bar of the House, by the by, is a line marked by a coloured strip of carpet on the floor of the Chamber beyond which MPs (or anyone for that matter) may not go when the Commons is sitting. Persons summoned to the Bar to give an account of themselves for contempt of Parliament are brought there by the Serjeant. On rare occasions when said person is likely to be stroppy, a brass rail is pulled across to make a more solid barrier.

If any MP wishes the House of Commons to go into a secret session, he calls out: 'Mr Speaker, I spy strangers.' A motion is then put to the House and if carried, the visitors' gallery and the press benches must be vacated.

A word which still causes some consternation when translated into the world's 3,000 languages is 'whip', which derives from fox-hunting, wherein 'whippers-in' are employed to regulate straying hounds. The duties of the whips are to ensure that MPs of their party attend vital votes (it is a word also used to describe a circular letter setting out important parliamentary business on which MPs must vote).

The 'woolsack' is worthy of a mention as in the House of Lords it is the equivalent of the Speaker's seat and is usually occupied by the Lord Chancellor. This is a relic of medieval times when a seat of sacks of wool underlined England's wealth.

Should an MP have had enough and wish to resign, he can apply for the position of 'Bailiff of the Chiltern Hundreds'. This is a technical procedural device by which an MP takes an 'office of profit under the Crown', which disqualifies him, or her, to sit as an MP. An alternative is the 'Stewardship of the Manor of Northstead', another Crown sinecure.

The Speaker is the 'chairman' of the House of Commons – his title comes from the days when someone was lumbered with telling the sovereign the wishes of Parliament. The position has been on the go since 1384, and as forthright monarchs have been known to execute Speakers it was not a job for which MPs clamoured. Hence, when a new Speaker is installed he puts up (a now mock) show of reluctance and has to be forced to occupy the Speaker's chair.

As general elections come and go, the British penchant for bringing their eccentricities to public knowledge increases and all over the United Kingdom weird candidates appear at the hustings. So far, these odd candidates have vied for the voters' favours: Freddie's Alternative Medicine Party; the Fancy Dress Party; Traditional English Food Party; the Nobody Party; the Monster Raving Looney Party – and not forgetting the party with the ultimate ace up their sleeve, the Jesus and His Cross Party.

9

THE HOSTESS GAME

From before the beginning of the reign of Queen Victoria, British 'polite society' was taken with the rituals of etiquette, those conventional forms of ceremony and decorum observed between equals. By the time Victoria passed to the great kingdom beyond, British etiquette was established in concrete and remained a mine-field for the unwary hostess. According to one Victorian rebel:

> Society is an elaborate, tiresome structure raised for the purpose of increasing needs and needlessly complicating life, inventing daily duties which do no good to anybody, and fostering in its hot, luxurious rooms, mean, ambitious and dangerous desires.

These obligations led to a busy day for the hostess who wanted to be recognised in society, and added to the British eccentricity of conforming to the need to be thought 'anyone'. The society ladies' day – and that of their drone-like menfolk who had nothing better to do – began with 'morning calls', at which tea and small-talk was dispensed. So that no one should put a foot wrong the (anonymous) author of *Society Small-Talk* (1879) gave a blow-by-blow set of hints on introductions:

> When the call is made and the visitor is ushered into the drawing room, and the hostess has risen to shake hands, the usual salutation should be, 'How do you do?' The abbreviation of 'How do you do?' into 'Howdy do?' is supposed by some to be the height of good manners, whereas it sounds affected and is rather in bad taste than not . . . The salutation 'How do you do?' should simply be regarded as a salutation only, and not as a personal enquiry after the health of the individual to whom it is addressed; and this formula of 'How do you do?' should be answered with the like formula of 'How do you do?'

Whether or not you liked tea was immaterial. The perfect hostess was duty-bound by the rules of politeness to press the visitor to even a single sip before she produced the family photograph album with dicky-bird attentive prints of the dead and not so alive. All in all, the morning call was to help show one's friends the scale of one's wealth.

The 'afternoon call' was a similar pressing obligation fraught with the juggling of handfuls of visiting cards. A lady when visiting, left such cards for herself and her husband. If the person called upon was 'not at home', that is, either genuinely out, or lurking behind the velvet curtains of the drawing-room, then the caller left three cards – one on behalf of herself and two for her husband (one from him to the husband and one from him to the wife). Cards were left even if the hostess was in. If grown-up daughters were present, the said caller turned down one corner of the visiting card to indicate their presence. Men callers were required to clutch their hats throughout tea, or place them where the servants could fall over them, or rest them on their knees as a suitable receptacle for uneaten buns, sandwiches, or unwanted fripperies.

In summer the afternoon call might turn into a garden party, where sherry or claret cup might also be given to guests, along with the obligatory music. One society hostess, Lady Beatrice Violet Greville, remarked in *The Gentlewoman in Society* (1892):

> Music at garden parties is usually confined to the braying of a military brass or the wild harmonies of a Hungarian band, the loud tones of which accord with the freedom of the open air and the want of attention likely to be given to the music. In shady nooks, or behind bushes, you may tumble upon Tyrolese singers, or ringers of handbells, surrounded by little groups of listeners which rapidly melt away.

Dinner parties were not designed to be enjoyed, but were events of reciprocal hospitality, or trading mutton chop for mutton chop. The hostess who wanted to make an impression stuck to the stomach-distending concoctions of Isabella Mary Beeton (1836–65), the writer on cookery who, with her *Book of Household Management* (1861), dug more graves with a knife and fork than the chief undertaker at Highgate Cemetery. They might even read the cookbook *Cook's Oracle* (with its chapter on 'How to Roast a Pound of Butter') by the eccentric Dr William Kitchener (d 1827) who spent most of his life dining.

Persons invited to his public dinners were urged to read the sign on the mantelpiece which read: 'Come at seven, go at eleven.'

On the marriage of her daughter, every caring society mother included in the trousseau a copy of *Hints on Etiquette* (1834) which recommended fifteen basic principles as fundamental to good 'breeding':

> In all cases, the observances of the Metropolis (as the seat of refinement) . . . [and by that they meant London] . . . should be received as the standard of good breeding.
> Never make acquaintance in coffee houses, or other public places. As no person who respects himself does so, you may reasonably suspect any advances made to you.
> Well-bred people arrive as nearly at the appointed dinner hour as they can. It is a very vulgar assumption of importance purposely to arrive half an hour behind time.
> It is considered vulgar to take fish, or soup, twice.
> Do not ask any lady to take wine, until you see she has finished her fish, or soup.
> Never use your knife to convey food to your mouth under any circumstances, it is unnecessary, and glaringly vulgar. Feed yourself with a fork, or spoon, nothing else, a knife is only to be used for cutting.
> Eat peas with a dessert spoon; and curry also.
> Making a noise in chewing, or breathing hard in eating, are both unseemly habits, and ought to be eschewed. Many people make a disgusting noise with their lips whilst taking soup – a habit which should be carefully avoided.
> Do not pick your teeth much at table, as, however satisfactory a practice to yourself, to witness it is not a pleasant thing.
> Ladies should never dine with their gloves on – unless their hands are not fit to be seen.
> Finger glasses, filled with warm water, come on with the dessert. Wet a corner of your napkin, wipe your mouth, then rinse your fingers but do not practise the filthy habit of gargling your mouth at table.
> If you are so unfortunate as to have contracted the low habit of smoking, be careful to practise it under certain restrictions; at least, so long as you are desirous of being considered fit for civilised society.
> Smoking in the streets, or in a theatre, is only practised by shop-boys, pseudo-fashionables, and the 'swell mob'.
> Men often think when they wear a fashionable cut throat, an embroidered waistcoat, with a profusion of chains and other trinkets, that they are well dressed, entirely overlooking the less obtrusive, but more certain, marks of

a refined taste. The grand points are – well-made shoes, clean gloves, a white pocket handkerchief, and, above all, an easy and graceful deportment.
Dance quietly, do not kick and caper about, nor sway your body to and fro: Dance only from the hips downwards.

To deviate from the mores of society was considered even more eccentric than the eccentricities of conforming. According to the rules as set out here, two forceful figures of history would have been deemed 'suspect'. Queen Victoria – or so averred Robert Cecil, 3rd Marquis of Salisbury – ate peas from a knife with great rapidity. And Benjamin Disraeli (1804–81, later Earl of Beaconsfield) in his early parliamentary days wore the most outrageous dress with 'a profusion of chains and other trinkets'.

Britain was full of hostesses who were strong characters in their own right.

One exception to the hostess who spent vast sums on entertaining was Venetia James (1855–1939) who, despite marrying a wealthy American, was parsimonious. It was her housekeeping system to send back to butcher and grocer alike any perishable leftovers from parties and expect a refund. Once, guests reported, ten people dined off a single chicken at a soirée given by Mrs James. A niece, too, averred that if any of the cat's milk was left it was used for guests' tea. Certainly if any of her servants fell ill, Mrs James sent for a veterinary surgeon as he was cheaper than a GP. Again, any dead birds in her garden were retrieved for the cat and due adjustment was made to the animal's meat allowance.

Adeline Brudenell, Countess of Cardigan, fell foul of Queen Victoria from the beginning of her social career. For her second marriage, Adeline espoused the Comte de Lancastre, a Portuguese grandee. She thereafter travelled under the anglicised name of 'Countess of Lancaster' and cut a dash in tight military trousers of scarlet and a leopard-skin cape. Queen Victoria was miffed as the 'Countess of Lancaster' was one of her travelling pseudonyms. Alas for her guests, Adeline had the disconcerting habit of climbing into a coffin she kept in her ballroom to see if it was still comfortable and asked her guests how she looked.

An anti-hostess of sorts was Lady Margaret-Ann Tyrrell who died in 1939. Her husband William

George, Baron Tyrrell, was the British ambassador in Paris (1928–34) and she showed little or no interest in planning his official functions. She spent most of her time writing a *History of the World*, part of which she wrote up a tree in the embassy gardens. When she wanted to summon a footman she emitted an ear-splitting whistle.

A form of etiquette which every man and woman had to learn was that expected at funerals. The funeral of Arthur Wellesley, Duke of Wellington, in 1852, set the trend in obsequies, although no one expected to mirror the very high standard of military ceremonial lavished on the cadaver of the 'Iron Duke'. Still, the unrelieved black and the macabre display of sombre magnificence and funeral etiquette is hard to understand today in its rigidity.

First – hours only after a demise – mourning cards had to be printed giving the deceased's status, natal details and the date, place and time of the funeral. Black-edged mourning paper was also ordered on which the deceased's relatives wrote epistles in black ink and signed with black sealing-wax, the latter being melted with black candles. Those in London society probably had an account with emporiums such as Jay's London General Mourning Warehouse established in 1841. Often mourners were hired to stand in funeral garb at the front door of the afflicted's house. Straw was often laid outside in the street so that the family's tender grief was not disturbed by the rattle of traffic. Even the door-knocker was swathed in black crêpe. The body, now achieving a respect that in many cases it never received in life, was bedecked for viewing by relatives – sometimes hired mourners called mutes would stand by the coffin in the parlour as a guard of honour.

The grandeur of the deceased's cortège depended upon the actual status and wherewithal of the family. Invariably the horses drawing the hearse were as well dressed as the mourners, with black ostrich feather plumes and saddle blankets of black edged with silver. All men who passed such a cortège doffed their hats. The pace was always slow so that the neighbours could appreciate the magnificence of the turn-out.

Etiquette demanded that a period of mourning be observed, depending upon the relationship between the mourner and the mourned. Mimicking Queen Victoria, who went into almost permanent mourning when Prince Albert died in 1861, a widow's mourning was of the deepest and longest. Many society magazines set out the etiquette of dress for mourning. *The Queen* magazine of 1880 advised this:

> For the first twelve months the dress and mantle must be of paramatta, the skirt covered with crêpe, put on in one piece, to within an inch of the waist; sleeves tight to the arm, body entirely covered with crêpe, tight-fitting lawn cuffs, and deep lawn collar; the mantle or jacket is of the same material as the dress, and very heavily trimmed with crêpe.

All of which the society lady followed rigorously.

The etiquette of adultery achieved a high peak during the reign of King Edward VII when society sinned with style. The stately homes of Britain became the nocturnal playgrounds of the highest in the land, and anything was permitted so long as the bedroom door was kept discreetly closed. The strictness of the moral code and etiquette dating from the late 1830s meant that the men of Victorian and Edwardian Britain could only find illicit sex among the poorer classes. Yet the special set who vacillated around Albert Edward, Prince of Wales, were, with his enthusiasm and indulgence, able to derive a code of etiquette which permitted adulterous relationships with 'gentlewomen' as long as no public (or drawing-room) scandal undermined the family unit. The etiquette could not apply to His Royal Highness himself, of course, as no women could sleep discreetly with Edward – everyone would guess. Edward, however, observed the rules of etiquette. He chose mature women who realised there could be no obvious gifts, display or social advancement. All arrangements for amorous excursions were made through his staff of courtiers. The lovely Mrs Alice Keppel was one of Edward's closest friends and his *maîtresse* from 1898 – she noted that it was the done etiquette to curtsey before getting into the royal bed.

At the 'at homes' it was safe enough to flirt, but more carnal activity needed some ingenuity. To have peace with one's *inamorata* was not easy but a hostess could arrange a double invitation for herself, or her guests, with adultery on their minds. In certain circumstances husbands could be sent on fishing or shooting expeditions so the wives were left at play with current boyfriends who stayed behind to 'volunteer' to play tennis or croquet. A hostess who approved of a liaison was a boon to have, for she could arrange that rooms could be discreetly allotted. Often husband and wife were given separate rooms, so the ardent swain had to make sure that he opened the right door when the last lady's maid had retired (servants were always a bind for the adulterous, as they were always around). Even the most cunning Lothario could slip up. Lord Charles Beresford, for instance, who was an erstwhile friend of Edward VII, caused great embarrassment when he crept into a dark bedroom thinking it was the one of his lover. He jumped into the vast bed shouting 'Cock-a-doodle-doo' and found himself on top of the Bishop of Chester and his wife!

The environment and code of conduct of this British 'polite society' has been swept away by two world wars. Nevertheless, the eccentricity of hospitality is still in the blood of many who entertain and occasionally a quirk is noticed to be savoured and recalled.

10

THE FANTASY WORLD OF HOMES AND FOLLIES

Many of Britain's eccentrics have had a mania for building, and one stands out more than any other. William John Cavendish Scott-Bentinck (1800–79), 5th Duke of Portland, withdrew more and more from society as time went by. He had been MP for King's Lynn from 1824 to 1826, and devoted the next fifty years or so to the improvement of Welbeck Abbey, his estate in Nottinghamshire; those 'improvements' were to be based on the most remarkable set of eccentric plans ever seen in Britain.

When Portland took over Welbeck Abbey in 1854 he began to go out of his way to avoid people and invariably only went out at night (he was preceded by an old woman with a lamp to light his way, but she had to keep a distance of 40yd (36m) in front of him). One room of Welbeck was filled with boxes of brown wigs, and the duke had quite a collection of false beards, moustaches and eyebrows for use as disguise.

Most of Portland's building schemes were underground, part of his plan to keep out of the public eye. Whenever he journeyed away from his estate he travelled in a closed waggonette and was driven to the local station through his private tunnel. Once at the station, the waggonette was loaded on to the train with the duke still inside. A large screen was built in the garden of his London house to prevent him from being seen by his neighbours.

By far the strangest feature of Welbeck Abbey was the network of rooms and tunnels beneath the grounds of his estate. One tunnel started below the kitchens and was set with railway tracks; by means of a heated truck the duke's food was transported to wherever he happened to be. The longest tunnel on the estate was over a mile (1.6km) long and wide enough for two carriages to pass and linked with the local village. Easily the most impressive of the duke's buildings was the 'riding house', an enormous glass-roofed erection measuring 396 × 108 × 50ft (121 × 33 × 15m). The second largest building of its kind in the world, the duke used it as a storage place for family portraits.

Portland spent more than £70,000 on gas and water installations and he employed around 15,000 workmen on his estate; besides their wages each workman was given a donkey for his own transportation around the estate and an umbrella for bad weather. As a part of off-duty entertainments for his workers, the duke constructed a roller-skating rink. The duke's underground ballroom, at 174ft (53m) in length, was large enough for 2,000 people and was served by a huge lift – but, of course, no one came!

Careful to protect his health, when the duke wandered around his estates he wore three pairs of socks, two overcoats, thick trousers (tied at the knee to keep them out of the mud) and an extra tall top hat.

On his death many speculated about his eccentricity. Some who knew the family said that the 5th duke went 'queer' because of a thwarted love affair. It appears that the duke had fallen in love with the famous actress and singer Fanny Kemble (1809–93), but a match between them was forbidden by his father the 4th duke. After Portland's death the only modern pictures found in his collection were portraits of Fanny.

Andrew Peterson, an eccentric retired barrister, built a 200ft (61m) tower of ferro-concrete at Sway, on the B3055 a few miles north-east of Lymington, Hampshire. In this tower Peterson declared that he was to be buried (he had to die first, he noted) and on the top of the tower a light had to be kindled. On Peterson's death the light was ignited but trouble began immediately. Ships at sea confused the light with the nearby lighthouse and complaints were received by the coastguards. The light was extinguished and the quirky barrister was buried elsewhere.

Near the Hampshire town of Alton, south-west of Aldershot, a somewhat unbalanced schoolmaster spent thirty years in planning and erecting a building in which no normal human being could live. It had passages which led nowhere and rooms without doors. Further, he forgot to put in a staircase, but his descendants were able to refit it as a village school.

Yet, despite all these curious buildings, foreigners look at the British as the most quirky animal lovers in the world, especially when it comes to follies associated with animals. Up and down the land are memorials and curious relics set up to honour a variety of quadrupeds. In Westminster Abbey, for instance, on the sarcophagus of the Countess of Sussex, who died in 1589, the memory of a porcupine is perpetuated at her request. And at Shugborough Park, 6 miles (10km) out of Stafford, alongside the triumphal arch in memory of the famous navigator Vice-Admiral George Anson (1697–1762), is the monument to a cat, Anson's companion on trips around the globe. It is thought that this cat was the first to voyage around the world.

At Manchester there is a memorial to a horse, dated 30 September 1843, which reads:

> Fallen from his fellow's side,
> The steed beneath is lying;
> In harness here he died;
> His only fault was dying.

There is hardly a stately home in Britain that does not have its horse memorial.

Memorials have led to great public controversy. Anti-vivisectionists erected a memorial to a mongrel in 1906, with the partisan message that the animal had been 'done to death' in a medical experiment without first being anaesthetised. So controversial did the issue become that there were demonstrations (medical students threatened to 'do the statue to death' with a sledge-hammer) in Trafalgar Square and questions were asked in the House of Commons. At length, Battersea Council decided that the memorial must go; the statue and epitaph were smashed in a stone-yard but the controversy raged for some time in the drawing-rooms of the main protagonists.

Not to be outdone by the follies of the rich, two London workmen set up their own folly in 1752 and it was placed on the wall of the George Inn, Wanstead. The two men were engaged on repairs to the inn and were caught eating a pilfered cherry pie. When they appeared before the magistrate he fined them half a guinea and they carved an inscription to commemorate the event:

IN MEMORY OF
YE CHERRY PEY
AS COST ½ A GUINEY
YE 17 OF JULY
THAT DAY WE HAD GOOD CHEER
HOPE TO DO SO MANY A YEAR

R.C.1752 D. TERRY

Yet to many the strangest memorial of all showed that British eccentricity was not dimmed one iota by service abroad. On the north-west frontier of India stands the memorial to 'high-kicking Bessie-Jane', a mule once used by the British Army. Living for kicks was this mule's philosophy and her memorial reads:

> This stone is erected in respectful memory of Bessie-Jane, one of the liveliest mules ever to make a British soldier resort to swearing. In her lifetime she kicked two colonels, two majors, two captains, three lieutenants, five sergeants, eleven corporals, eighteen privates and, alas, one live grenade. It may truly be said that she kicked her way through life and into death.

11

CURIOUS COMPULSIONS

Sentimentality in the British character approaches eccentric proportions, especially when it concerns romanticism and the curious compulsions of supernatural belief. William Wordsworth (1770–1850), the English poet, formed an attachment to a gate. This was the Wishing Gate at Grasmere on the Ambleside road. Tradition attributed to it the power of fulfilling the desires of those who touched it three times as they stated their wishes out loud.

On hearing that the beloved gate had been torn off its hinges in 1842, Wordsworth wrote these lines to append to his poem *'The Wishing Gate'*:

> Tis gone – with old belief and dream
> That round it clung, and tempting scheme
> Released the bright landscape too must lie,
> By this blank wall, from every eye,
> Relentlessly shut out.

Yet he had been misinformed, so Wordsworth commented thus:

> Having been told, upon what I thought good authority, that this gate had been destroyed, and the opening where it hung walled up, I gave vent to my feelings in these stanzas. But going to the place some time after, I found, with much delight, my old favourite unmolested. W.

Finchdale Priory, sheltered by the precipitous crags of Cocken, County Durham, drew many a woman who feared herself barren. The object of relief was set on the sill of the oriel window of the prior's study in this monastic house once known as a monks' holiday retreat. On the sill were carved the outlines of a foot and a hand. In order to win the strange carving's benediction, the appellant had to climb on to the sill and place the left foot and the right hand in the corresponding depressions in the stone. Local chronicles record that the back-breaking rite was successful for women from all over Durham.

At Gourock, in the modern district of Inverclyde, there stands a monolith called 'Granny Kempock', much frequented in past years by those suffering from 'a broken heart'; a touch of 'Granny' restored the heart to its equanimity. Set in Kempock Street, overlooking the Clyde, this ancient standing stone, according to the tourist handbook, is no longer regarded with superstition. Yet in the folklore of Gourock, 'Granny' has been associated with both witchcraft and sea disasters (those who set sail sought first the blessing from 'Granny'), and occasionally she is still dressed at Hogmanay (Scotland's New Year revels). And a scene of eccentric behaviour might still be witnessed; as the late-night carouser scurries up to the wind-blown tenements, should a chill be caused to the spine by the witching-hour, one can always call out (as most folk did) 'Good night, Granny!' as one hurries breathlessly past.

The curious dance of love has brought out much eccentricity in Britons down the centuries, and at Crawl Meadows, Downton, Shropshire, an eccentric local tradition lives in memory. It perpetuates the remembrance of the young girl from the neighbouring village of Bromfield who fell for a youth from Downton. Her father refused to give his consent to the marriage, and the girl pleaded that she would do anything to win her father's permission. In exasperation at her nagging, he said that she could marry if she crawled all the way to her lover in Bromfield. She set off on her hands and knees and got as far as modern Crawl Meadows, where she collapsed; yet she made to go on. Impressed with her determination, her father relented and gave his consent.

But then, the traditions and rituals of the British have always led to quirky behaviour. Whether it was 'Trussing the Cooper' (an apprentice cooper was lowered into a burning barrel) at Mortlake, or shaking hands with a chimney-sweep (the traditional bearer of good fortune) at a wedding, the British have forged down the years the greatest collection in the world of eccentric trades, social and seasonal customs. So when foreigners see wedding cake being crumbled over the head of a bride on Holy Island, or shot-guns being fired over the bridal party in Northumberland, they think the worst!

12

A POET, A DUKE AND A PARCEL OF DONS

St Andrews, Scotland's oldest university, has produced more academic eccentrics per capita than any other north of the Border. One St Andrews academic who was a living legend in his day, also qualified as the most absent-minded of all professors. He was Professor George Frederick Stout (1860–1944), who held the Chair of Logic and Metaphysics.

Stout, it is said, once had a lecture engagement at Edinburgh. He boarded the train at St Andrews, but by the time he had reached Leuchars Junction (4 miles (6km) away), where he had to change trains, he had forgotten where he was going. Luckily, he remembered his wife's name and his address and telephoned her to ask where he was going. His wife said: 'Look at your return ticket.' Stout looked at the return half of his ticket and caught the next train back to St Andrews.

Another colourful don from St Andrews, and one who commanded great respect, was Professor Sir D'Arcy Wentworth Thompson (1860–1948). An internationally known naturalist, D'Arcy Thompson was a well-known figure. He was frequently seen walking around St Andrews wearing white sand-shoes and with a bird of prey on his shoulder – to the delight of small children and to the terror of wilting spinsters.

D'Arcy Thompson was a classics scholar as well as a naturalist, and there must be something about classics in the eccentric scheme of things, because another curious St Andrews academic was the poet and polymath Professor Douglas Young (1913–73). A very tall, bearded man – his students referred to him as 'Jesus Christ' – Young was a fervent Scottish Nationalist. A conscientious objector in World War II, he was serenaded outside his cell by groups of SNP supporters, but more than that, Young summed up all that is and was 'Scottish eccentricity' in that he was an individual. For, among the Celts, the Scots are he most individualistic and will brook no criticism of heir history, religion, or sporting activities.

An academic of a different sort was James Burnett, ,ord Monboddo (1714–99), who was admitted to the Scottish bar in 1737. Full of whimsicalities, Monboddo believed that all babies were born with tails and hat midwives spirited the tails away in a conspiracy of silence. Monboddo, in his book *The Origin of Progress and Language*, considered it likely that orang-outangs could be trained to speak Greek, his favourite language.

Greek life was Monboddo's passion and for many years he held what was known as 'learned suppers'. Herein the intelligentsia dined in Attic fashion, from a table strewn with roses in the manner of Horace at his home in the Sabine hills, and drank from wine flagons garlanded like Anacreon's at the court of Polycrates of Samos. One day, a friend related, he saw the learned lawman come out of Edinburgh's Court of Session. On seeing that it was raining, Monboddo put his wig into his sedan chair and walked home himself in the rain.

Alexander Douglas-Hamilton, 10th Duke of Hamilton and 7th Duke of Brandon, was perhaps the most consistently eccentric of the Scottish noble lords. The mantle of nobility lay heavily on his shoulders; he was also Marquess of Clydesdale, Earl of Angus and of Arran, Lanark and Cambridge, a peer three times over and a baron. To anyone who would listen, he explained why he was the true heir to the Scottish throne. He claimed that soon after his birth at Edinburgh Castle in 1566, James VI was murdered and a changeling substituted. Consequently he, Alexander, should be king as the line would descend through the Douglas family. The Hanoverian incumbents of the British throne thought naught of the noble duke's claims. Yet Hamilton treated any visitors royally, especially when they visited his home on the Isle of Arran; in fact, all visitors to the island were given carte blanche to wine, dine and be accommodated entirely at the duke's expense.

Perhaps his greatest eccentricity was his concern for and with his last resting place. The duke first turned his mind to the casket in which he was to be buried. To this end he outbid the agents of the British Museum and bought, for £11,000, the sarcophagus of an Egyptian princess. On arrival at Hamilton Palace (the treasures of the palace were dispersed in 1882 and the house long demolished because of coal-working subsidence) the sarcophagus was found to be too short; but, on his deathbed the duke, ever anxious gave orders to be lifted into the sarcophagus to test its length again. It was still too short. 'Double me up Double me up!' was his last command.

Alas, the duke could not be accommodated in the tomb whole, so his feet were cut off and placed in the tomb separately. The duke's last journey had been to collect the spices with which he was to be embalmed and he was entombed as a great patrician. Alas again, the duke's sarcophagus was found to be that not of a princess, but a court jester!

The duke's last resting place was a 120ft high (36m) mausoleum with a stone cupola in the classic style by David Bryce, erected by the said Alexander Hamilton for £130,000. The interior is a solemn octagonal chapel, where voices arouse a long-drawn out and dulcet echo, intoning perhaps the 10th duke's words 'Oh! what a grand sight it will be, when twelve Dukes of Hamilton rise together here at the Resurrection!' Needless to say, when studying the 10th duke's track record, the vaults beneath the inlaid marble lie empty, and the bronze doors of the mausoleum copied from Ghiberti's of the Baptistry at Florence, add only to the great folly which thunders with the heavy profane traffic on the M74.

No comment on Scottish eccentrics could ever be complete without a mention of William McGonagall (1825–1902). Born in Dundee and employed in a hand-loom mill, McGonagall discovered that he was a 'poet' in 1877. His first effort was to show that his talent was as eccentric as his person. The poem appeared in the Dundee *Weekly News* and set McGonagall on the road to being Britain's worst poet. This first 'masterpiece' celebrated the faith and oratory of the Reverend George Gilfillan, and began:

Rev George Gilfillan of Dundee,
There is none can you excel;
You have boldly rejected the Confession of Faith,
And defended your cause right well.

The first time I heard him speak,
'Twas in the Kinnaird hall,
Lecturing on the Garibaldi movement,
As loud as he could bawl.

McGonagall believed that his gift should reach the highest in the land, so he wrote a 'Requisition to the Queen' asking her to accept his poems. In replying to McGonagall, Sir Thomas Biddulph, Master of the Household, said that the queen could not possibly accept McGonagall's verses. This, however, fired the Dundonian with inspiration, and styling himself 'Poet to Her Majesty', he set off for the queen's Scottish residence of Balmoral. 'My far-famed Balmoral journey', as McGonagall called it, was not a success as he was turned away at the porter's lodge.

Nevertheless, the awful standard of his poetry and the eccentricity of his public readings won him immortality in the annals of Scottish eccentricity. McGonagall believed that the appointment of Alfred Tennyson (1809–92) as poet laureate had been granted by pure influence and not talent, and that he, McGonagall, was more fitting to succeed William Wordsworth. Consequently he always aimed high and his last poem, written only weeks before he died, was in honour of the coronation of Edward VII with the unforgettable lines!

'Twas in the year of 1902, and on August the 9th,
a beautiful day,
That thousands of people came from far away,
All in a state of excitement and consternation,
Resolved to see King Edward the VII's Coronation.

13

HOW TO BE A MODERN ECCENTRIC

> Eccentricity has always abounded when and where strength of character has abounded; and the amount of eccentricity in a society has been proportional to the amount of genius, mental vigour, and moral courage it contained. (John Stuart Mill, *On Liberty*)

English philosophers like Mill have long averred that eccentricity in a nation is a downright necessity for the survival of that nation as an independent entity. Every society has its 'norms' and there will always be those who try to break away; Russian labour camps are full of such people. On a more homely note take the case of the lady who was recently successful in petitioning the Planning Committee of Exeter City Council not to permit the building of some houses next to hers. She averred that she was a witch and that the houses would interfere with her flight path to Dartmoor, her coven's place of assignation!

Although most of us are reluctant to behave *too* eccentrically, there are steps which can be taken to add a little eccentricity to life.

Step One: Acquire unconventionality

Unless you become unconventional you cannot hope to understand eccentricity. This first step towards success can be achieved in a number of ways. Dress and food habits are good examples of subjects to start with, and are more potent if they can be combined. If, for instance, you can acquire the taste for kippers spread with jam for your breakfast – eaten at your own fireside while you sit, say, in your silk dressing-gown over jodhpurs and topped with a tartan night-cap – then you are beginning to be unconventional.

Step Two: Become a good 'turn'

This may require you to make a fool of yourself in public, at the same time as acting as if *you* do not see anything strange in your behaviour. This could incur such needs as using your front garden as a loo if you are doing some weeding and your statutory lavatory (a trainee-eccentric never says 'toilet') is too far away. All in all, you must make your presence felt in company, carefully avoiding fashionable mores.

Step Three: Be a true snob
Now, that does not mean that you have to look down on people; it means assessing things according to their intrinsic value. Remember, the true snob on his way to eccentricity and the dubious values of the *nouveau riche* can be spotted immediately. By way of example, say you were to choose as a gift between two Victorian tumblers: one that was used by Queen Victoria to drink wine out of, another that was used by her for her false teeth. The *nouveau riche* would take the first and the neophyte eccentric the latter.

Step Four: Cultivate imagination
In the world of the true eccentric it is quite wrong to include such people as, say, witches or freaks, as they are not pure eccentrics. For eccentricity only suggests minor deviations from the norm; anything else containing madness or criminality is not eccentricity at all. So it is necessary to try doing things in an odd or quirky manner with imagination and humour. The whole key is individuality and has nothing to do with riches – the real eccentric lives his life with distinctiveness, whilst the rich man has no more than self-indulgence. Note how, down the centuries, too, people from clergymen to tramps, and from academics to odd-job men have made ideal eccentrics because the lives they led gave them a freedom to behave in a contrary fashion. So the prospering of eccentricity may entail a change of job, for it is easier for a gamekeeper in the Highlands of Scotland to be eccentric than a mortgage-laden executive from Surbiton. But the cultivation of imagination, and *per se* a knowledge of the world of fantasy, must be tempered with care. For too much leads to pseudo-eccentricity like that of J. M. Barrie who, like Peter Pan, just did not grow up; or Kenneth Grahame who, in writing *The Wind in the Willows*, showed that he could never quite face up to the adult world.

Being imaginative can be enhanced if you add somehow to the country's traditions. William Strickland, the explorer, for instance, invited his friends around for dinner at Christmas 1523, on his return from America. The chief course at the festive meal was a strange bird, which the company ate roasted. So, with a little imagination, Strickland invented the traditional Christmas dinner of turkey.

Step Five: Learn to talk with wit

The world's top eccentrics are undoubtedly good conversationalists, so that the acquiring of a witty manner in conversation is a must, especially if this can be added to a discursive authority about any subject. That topic, however, must have an originality bordering on an obsession – sport is out as there are too many sporting bores around, and eccentrics must never be boring. This does not mean either that one has to mimic the like of Cardinal Giuseppe Mezzofanti (1774–1849), a Vatican librarian who was reputed to have spoken thirty-nine tongues with a knowledge of eleven other spoken languages.

Over and above these five main steps to success as an eccentric may be added an 'optional extra' – the habits of a recluse. Down the centuries men and women, for religious reasons – which may or may not be considered eccentric, depending upon one's religious beliefs – have become recluses. Others who saw nothing much in the world to attract them have retired behind their own four walls. One man who had the world at his feet is now taking on the character of an eccentric recluse.

Former Beatle, George Harrison, who has mixed the life of a hippie with that of a multi-millionaire, bought a Gothic mansion called Friar Park, Henley-on-Thames, Oxfordshire, to be his hermitage in 1969. This shy, quirky musician follows all of his interests these days behind closed doors in almost total secrecy. Even his gate has 'no admittance' signs in ten languages. The mansion itself is used to odd behaviour as it once belonged to the eccentric philanthropist Sir Frank Crisp who built it in horror-movie style in 1896. Harrison, it is said, has spent £1½ million restoring the mansion to its eccentric glory.

The seeds of eccentricity are alive and well throughout Britain. So, encourage an eccentric and add to the nation's survival in a Europe of conformity.